PIANO/VOCAL SELECTIONS

Hal Luftig   Fox Theatricals   Dori Berinstein

James L. Nederlander   Independent Presenters Network   Roy Furman   Amanda Lipitz
Broadway Asia   Barbara Whitman   FWPM Group   Hendel/Wiesenfeld
Goldberg/Binder   Stern/Meyer   Lane/Comley   Bartner-Jenkins/Nocciolino
and Warren Trepp

In Association with MGM ON STAGE Darcie Denkert and Dean Stolber

Present

Music and Lyrics by   Book by
LAURENCE O'KEEFE and NELL BENJAMIN   HEATHER HACH

BASED UPON THE NOVEL BY AMANDA BROWN
and THE METRO-GOLDWYN-MAYER MOTION PICTURE

Starring

LAURA BELL BUNDY

CHRISTIAN BORLE   ORFEH

RICHARD H. BLAKE   KATE SHINDLE   NIKKI SNELSON

and MICHAEL RUPERT

With

ANNALEIGH ASHFORD   APRIL BERRY   PAUL CANAAN   LINDSAY NICOLE CHAMBERS   BETH CURRY
TRACY JAI EDWARDS   AMBER EFÉ   GAELEN GILLILAND   JASON GILLMAN   BECKY GULSVIG
ROD HARRELSON   MANUEL HERRERA   NATALIE JOY JOHNSON   ANDY KARL   NICK KENKEL
MICHELLE KITTRELL   LESLIE KRITZER   DeQUINA MOORE   RUSTY MOWERY   KEVIN PARISEAU
MATTHEW RISCH   JASON PATRICK SANDS   NOAH WEISBERG   KATE WETHERHEAD

Produced for Fox Theatricals by

KRISTIN CASKEY and MIKE ISAACSON

Scenic Design	Costume Design	Lighting Design	Sound Design
DAVID ROCKWELL	GREGG BARNES	KEN POSNER & PAUL MILLER	ACME SOUND PARTNERS

Casting	Hair Design	Associate Director	Associate Choreographer
TELSEY + COMPANY	DAVID BRIAN BROWN	MARC BRUNI	DENIS JONES

Technical Supervisor	Animal Trainer	Production Stage Manager	General Management
SMITTY/THEATERSMITH, INC.	WILLIAM BERLONI	BONNIE L. BECKER	NLA/MAGGIE BROHN

Press Agent	Marketing	Associate Producers
BARLOW•HARTMAN	TMG-THE MARKETING GROUP	PMC PRODUCTIONS YASUHIRO KAWANA ANDREW ASNES/ADAM ZOTOVICH

Music Director/Conductor	Orchestrations	Arrangements	Music Contractor
JAMES SAMPLINER	CHRISTOPHER JAHNKE	LAURENCE O'KEEFE & JAMES SAMPLINER	MICHAEL KELLER

Directed and Choreographed by

JERRY MITCHELL

Cover photo © Kate Turning

Translation of "Ireland" by Bairbre Finn

ISBN 978-1-4234-5912-5

A RODGERS AND HAMMERSTEIN COMPANY

www.williamsonmusic.com

EXCLUSIVELY DISTRIBUTED BY

HAL•LEONARD
CORPORATION

7777 W. BLUEMOUND RD. P.O. BOX 13819 MILWAUKEE, WI 53213

Visit Hal Leonard Online at
www.halleonard.com

NELL BENJAMIN AND LAURENCE O'KEEFE

Nell has just finished a disturbingly free adaptation of Gilbert and Sullivan's *The Pirates of Penzance* called *Pirates! (or Gilbert and Sullivan plunder'd)* which was a commercial and critical success at the Goodspeed Opera House and the Paper Mill Playhouse.

Before eviscerating classics of English operetta, Nell wrote *Cam Jansen and the Curse of the Emerald Elephant*, with Laurence O'Keefe. Produced by TheatreworksUSA at the Lamb's Theater, *Cam* was nominated for a 2005 Drama Desk Award for Best Book of a Musical. Nell wrote lyrics for *Sarah, Plain and Tall* and *The Mice*, which was nominated for an Ovation Award. Nell and Larry also contributed a song for TheatreworksUSA's latest review *If You Give a Pig a Pancake*. The song, based on the children's book "How I Became a Pirate," continues the pirate theme that runs through her work. Her work for television includes the last and weirdest season of *Unhappily Ever After* and Animal Planet's *Whoa! Sunday with Mo Rocca*.

She holds an M.Phil. from University of Dublin, Trinity College and a B.A. from Harvard University. She is the recipient of the 2003 Kleban Foundation Award for lyrics and a 2003 Jonathan Larson Foundation grant. She is a member of ASCAP and the Dramatists Guild of America.

Larry also wrote music and lyrics for *Bat Boy: The Musical*, which originated at the Actors Gang Theater in Los Angeles, won two Richard Rodgers Awards from the American Academy of Arts and Letters, and was produced Off-Broadway, winning the Lucille Lortel and Outer Critics' Circle Awards for Best Off-Broadway Musical as well as Drama Desk Award nominations for Best Musical, Best Music and Best Lyrics. *Bat Boy* has been produced in London's West End, the Edinburgh Fringe Festival, in Tokyo, Korea, Berlin and over 300 other productions worldwide. Larry has written songs and scores for "The Daily Show," Disney's "Johnny and the Sprites" and PBS's documentary "Make 'Em Laugh." He has won the Kleban Foundation Award, the ASCAP Richard Rodgers New Horizon Award, a Jonathan Larson Foundation grant and USC's Harry Warren Prize. Larry studied anthropology at Harvard University and film scoring at Berklee College of Music and the University of Southern California.

Nell and Larry's work on *Legally Blonde* received a 2007 Tony® Award nomination for Best Score, 2007 Drama Desk Award nominations for music and lyrics, and the Broadway.com Audience Award for Best Song. They live in New York, while in Los Angeles they own two cars and some furniture and stuff, but no house.

OMIGOD YOU GUYS

Music and Lyrics by LAURENCE O'KEEFE
and NELL BENJAMIN

9

SERENA: *Guys, she's not here.*
DELTA NUS: *(confused hubbub)*
MARGO: *Bruiser, where's Elle?*
BRUISER: *(Yaps)*
MARGOT: *She realized she doesn't have an engagement outfit?*
BRUISER: *(Yaps)*

MARGOT: *She's totally freaking out?!*
BRUISER: *(Yaps)*
MARGOT: *She's trapped in the old valley mill?!*
BRUISER: *(Yaps)*
MARGOT: *(relieved) Oh sorry, the Old Valley Mall.*
(All relieved, then suddenly gasp.)

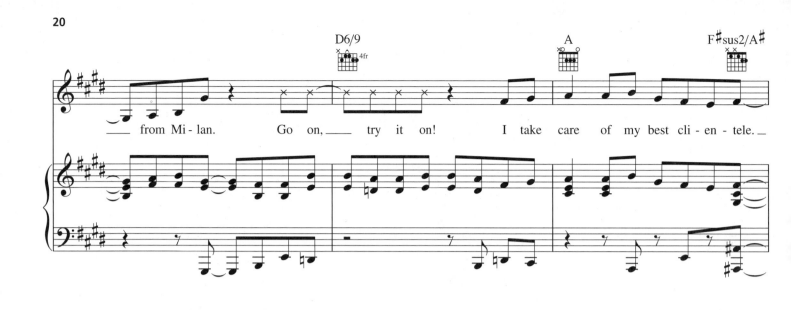

from Mi - lan. Go on,___ try it on! I take care of my best cli - en - tele.___

It's a gift from me___ to Elle!___

ALL GIRLS:

Ah!___

Slower

ELLE:

Oh my God!___ O - mi - god, you guys!___

Ah!___ ah ah ___

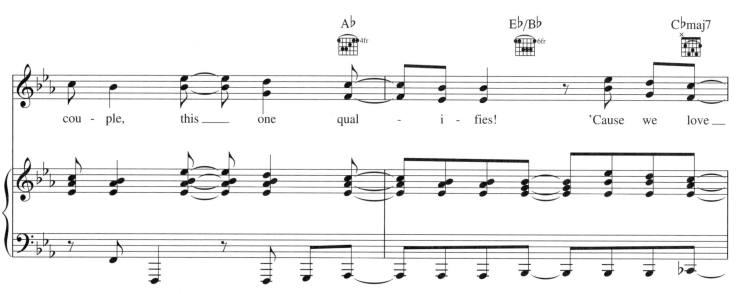

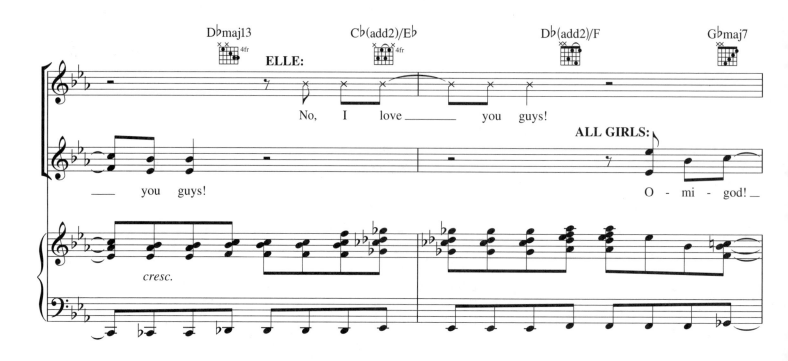

SERIOUS

Music and Lyrics by LAURENCE O'KEEFE
and NELL BENJAMIN

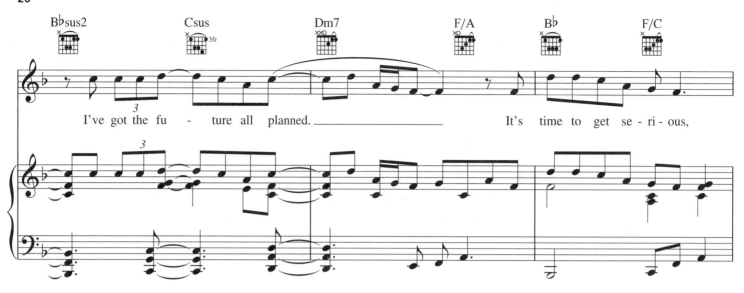

I've got the fu - ture all planned. _____ It's time to get se - ri - ous,

time to get se - ri - ous with you. _____

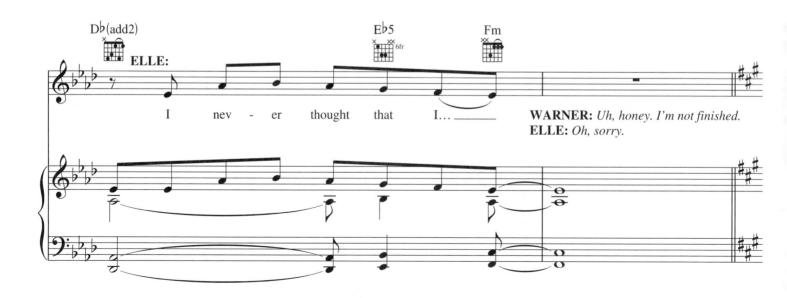

ELLE: I nev - er thought that I... _____

WARNER: *Uh, honey. I'm not finished.*
ELLE: *Oh, sorry.*

WHAT YOU WANT

Music and Lyrics by LAURENCE O'KEEFE
and NELL BENJAMIN

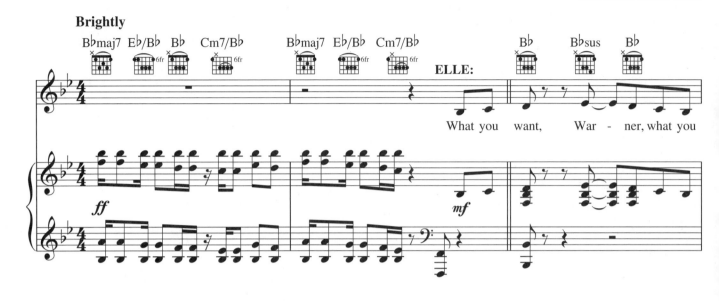

Brightly

ELLE:

What you want, War - ner, what you

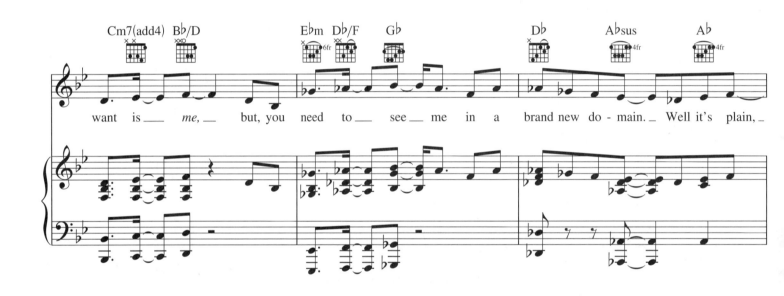

want is __ me, __ but, you need to __ see __ me in a brand new do - main. __ Well it's plain, __

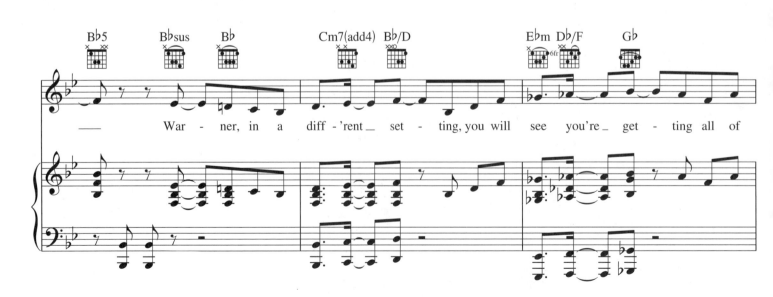

__ War - ner, in a diff -'rent __ set - ting, you will see you're get - ting all of

*Margot, Pilar & Serena

film ca - reer? How 'bout a nice Bir-kin bag? Yes! The East Coast is for-eign: there's no

film stu - di - os. ___ It's cold and dark, no val - et park - ing, all the girls have dif - f'rent nos - es.

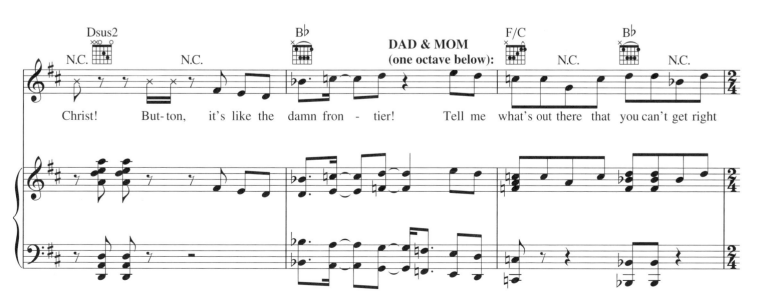

Christ! But-ton, it's like the damn fron - tier! Tell me what's out there that you can't get right

_____ What U want, U wan-na be prov-in' sum-pin', and to whom?_ What U want, U wan-na be

won-drin' where _ youth is gone?___ What U want? U wan-na hold on! **ELLE:** Hold on. **BOYS:** Whoa!_

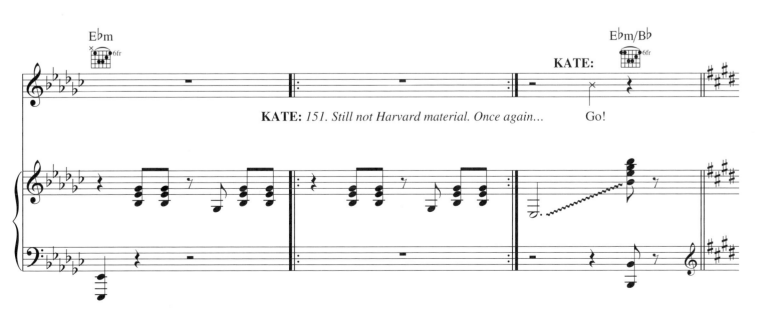

KATE: *151. Still not Harvard material. Once again…* **KATE:** Go!

Moderato, Ballad

Stadium Rock Ballad

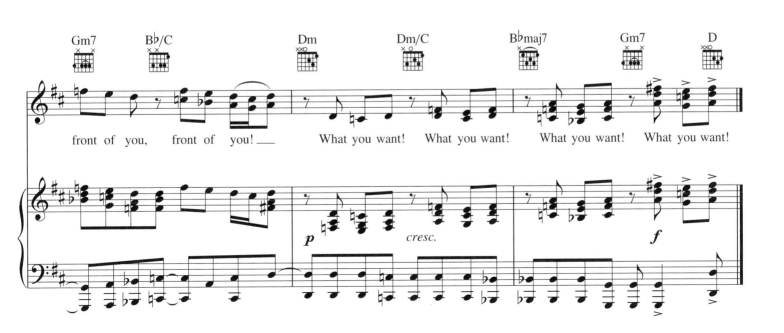

POSITIVE

Music and Lyrics by LAURENCE O'KEEFE
and NELL BENJAMIN

Hon-ey, what you cry-in' at? __ You're not los-in' him __ to that. __

Both her hair and shoes are flat! __ And why is she __ so rude?

Wipe your tears, it's no __ big thing. __ You were meant to wear __ his ring! __

SERENA: You will whet his ap-pe-tite! __

MARGOT: You and he will re-u-nite! __

add PILAR & SERENA: You know we're right!

GREEK CHORUS: We're pos - i - tive! _____ We're pos - i -

tive! _____ We're pos - i - tive! _____ We're pos - i...

ELLE: *Oh my God, you're making me sick.*

VIVIENNE: *Are we? Warner, let's take this back to my place.*

GREEK CHORUS: Ah. _____ Hey!

IRELAND

Music and Lyric by LAURENCE O'KEEFE
and NELL BENJAMIN

68

SO MUCH BETTER

Music and Lyric by LAURENCE O'KEEFE
and NELL BENJAMIN

WHIPPED INTO SHAPE

Music and Lyric by LAURENCE O'KEEFE
and NELL BENJAMIN

Big fat commercial Pop-Funk

BROOKE:

Do you want an eas-y mir-a-cle?_ Do you wan-na lose a pound or two? Then you can turn_ this off right now, my work-out's not for you._ I'm talk-in' to the wom-an who wants it all._ Got-ta

teen nine - ty nine! You'll have him whipped in - to shape! When you get grief from a guy, just work him

o - ver with this 'til he starts to ___ cry. If he don't act like he should, you got to

whip it, whip it, whip it good! It gets you out of an - y scrape, ___ and gets you whipped in - to shape!

Whipped in - to shape!

TAKE IT LIKE A MAN

Music and Lyric by LAURENCE O'KEEFE
and NELL BENJAMIN

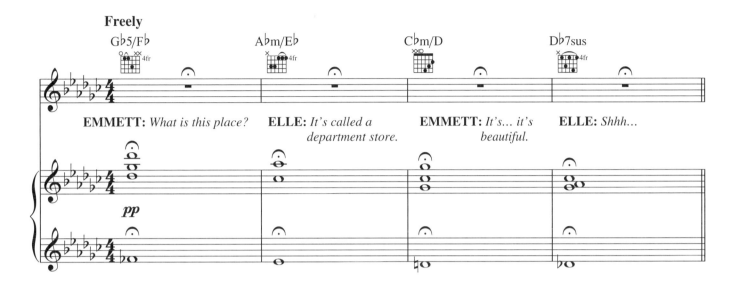

Freely

EMMETT: *What is this place?*   ELLE: *It's called a department store.*   EMMETT: *It's... it's beautiful.*   ELLE: *Shhh...*

pp

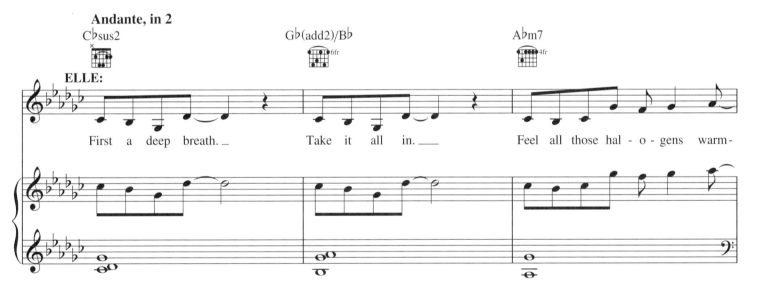

Andante, in 2

ELLE:

First a deep breath. _ Take it all in. _ Feel all those hal - o - gens warm-

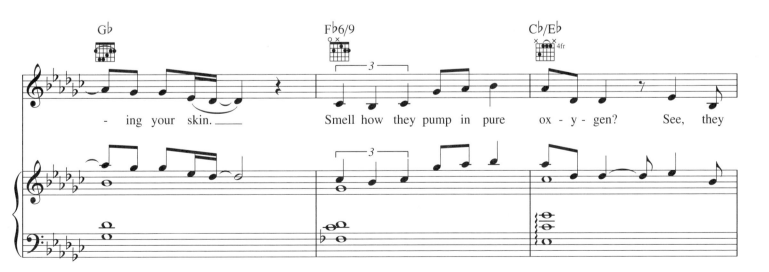

- ing your skin. _ Smell how they pump in pure ox - y - gen? See, they

Not quite the guy I'd-a chose __ to be. __ But when she's stand - ing so close __

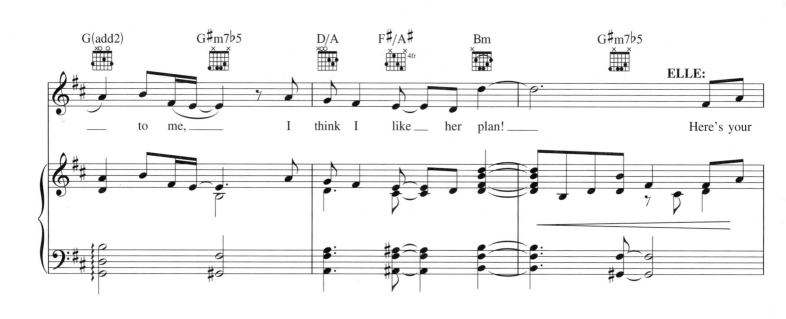

__ to me, __ I think I like __ her plan! __ Here's your

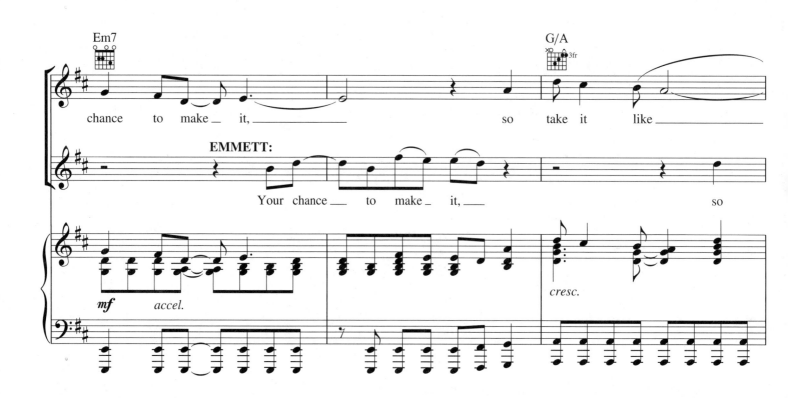

chance to make __ it, __ so take it like __

Your chance __ to make __ it, __ so

BEND AND SNAP

Music and Lyric by LAURENCE O'KEEFE
and NELL BENJAMIN

*Elle, Serena, Margot and Pilar

108

THERE! RIGHT THERE!

Music and Lyric by LAURENCE O'KEEFE
and NELL BENJAMIN

Tarantella, in 2

ELLE: There! Right there! Look at that tan, well-tend - ed skin! Look at the

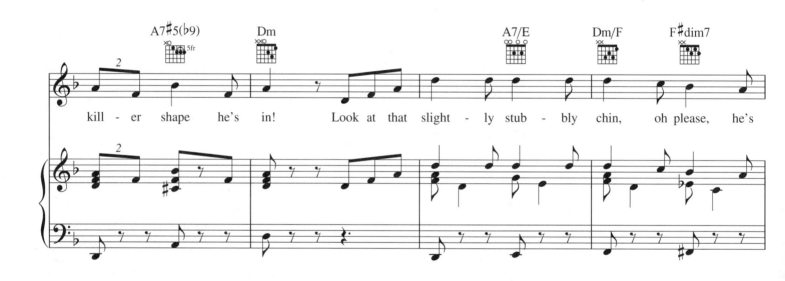

kill - er shape he's in! Look at that slight - ly stub - bly chin, oh please, he's

CALLAHAN: gay, to - tal - ly gay! I'm not a - bout to cel - e - brate. Ev - er - y

114

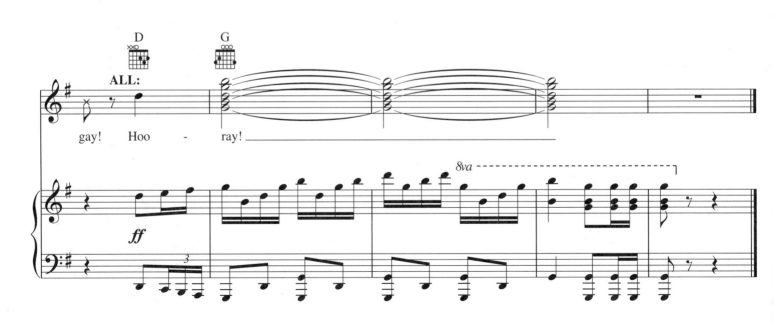

LEGALLY BLONDE

Music and Lyric by LAURENCE O'KEEFE
and NELL BENJAMIN

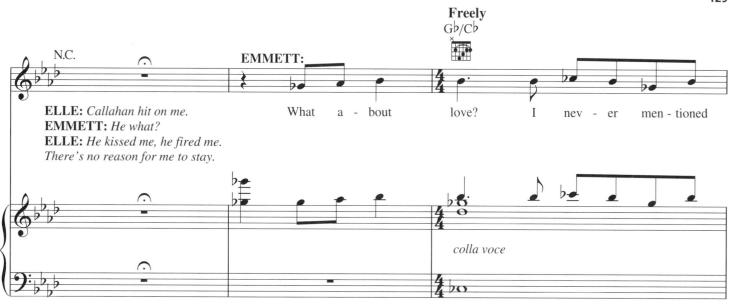

ELLE: *Callahan hit on me.*
EMMETT: *He what?*
ELLE: *He kissed me, he fired me.*
There's no reason for me to stay.

EMMETT: What a-bout love? I nev-er men-tioned

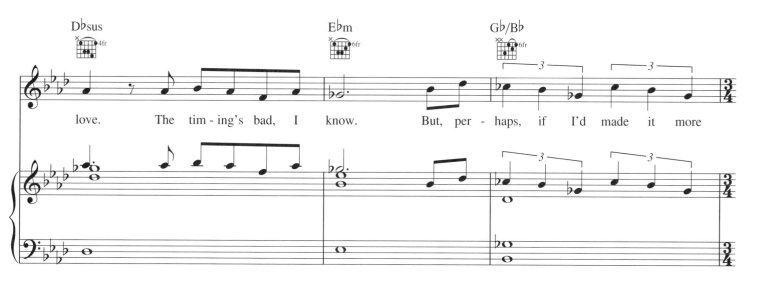

love. The tim-ing's bad, I know. But, per-haps, if I'd made it more

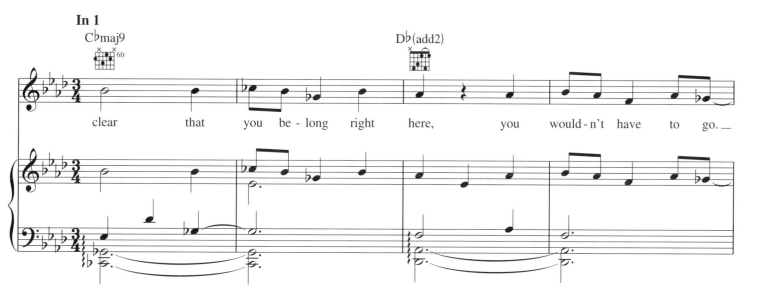

clear that you be-long right here, you would-n't have to go. __

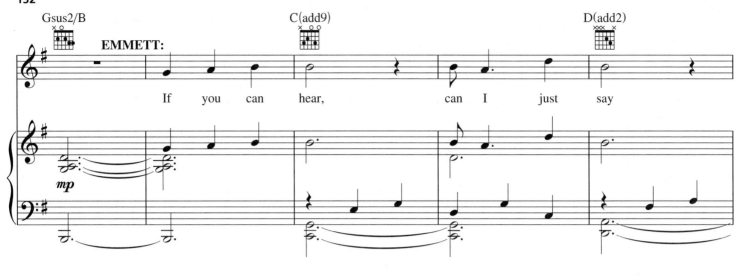

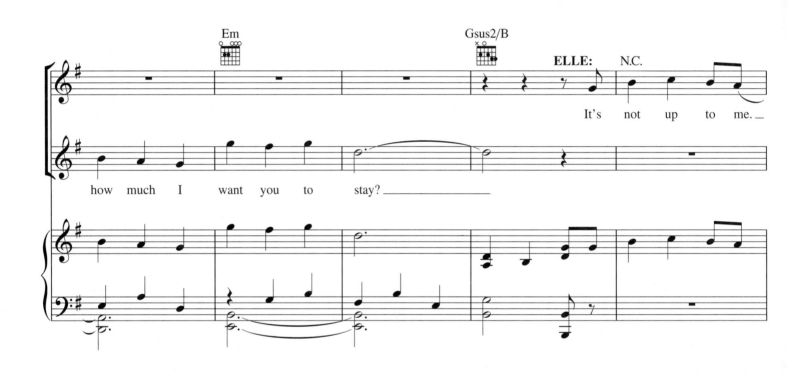

LEGALLY BLONDE REMIX

Music and Lyric by LAURENCE O'KEEFE
and NELL BENJAMIN

C6   F(add2)

_and, as a rule, ___ I do not bond. ___

Ab   Dbmaj9   Eb6   Fm7

_But, I see a star, ___ you're my new muse; ___ you've got the best_

Ab(add2)/C   Gbmaj9

_frick-in shoes! ___ And you lit a fuse, ___ so go show 'em who's_

Db   Ab(add2)   Fm7   Gbmaj7

_le-gal-ly blonde! ___ Yes, you lit a fuse, _

Get on your feet 'cause she's le - gal - ly blonde! _____ Take to the street 'cause she's

le - gal - ly blonde! _____ There's no re - treat when you're le - gal - ly blonde! _ Yeah!

Aah, _____

Aah, _____